# THIS JOURNAL BELONGS TO

_____

_____

_____

# My Badass Gratitude Journal

ISBN -13: 979-8-218-00453-8

R
Regan Press

# MY BADASS GRATITUDE JOURNAL

A MAGICAL JOURNEY OF APPRECIATION
TO ACTUALLY HELP YOU LIVE A
BLISSFUL, INSPIRED, GRATEFUL LIFE.

SHEILA KAMUDA

R
Regan Press

# My Badass Gratitude Journal

## A magical journey of appreciation to actually help you live a blissful, inspired, Grateful life.

Packed with 52 guided prompts, inspirational quotes, and a Gratitude Manifesto broken down into 10 principles, this journal is all about appreciation. And it starts with YOU.

## About the Author

Sheila Kamuda is a writer, speaker, success coach, and founder of Live Out Loud Coaching. Her first journal, *My Badass Journal*, is a discovery of self-love. She created *My Badass Gratitude Journal* to show you the magic of living a life of appreciation, starting with you.

Sheila Kamuda
Live Out Loud Coaching

# For Sydney,

*whose free spirit,*
*belief in self and love of life*
*always shines a light for me.*

# PROLOGUE

It might be one of the hardest things to do. I'm talking about being grateful for you. It's hard to turn inward and thank ourselves for us.

We're taught that it's boastful so we shy away from it. And all that's done is make us feel unworthy. It's caused self- doubt. It's made us compare ourselves to others. It's made us loathe parts of ourselves. It's made us feel small.

So here's an opportunity to turn that around. To start your gratitude journey with being thankful for you. Every inch of you. Every cell in your body. Every aspect of your fabulous Badass self.

Once you get the hang of this, it won't be so hard. I mean how can you be grateful for the things or people around you if you aren't grateful for you? So let's change that.

# Badass GRATITUDE manifesto

Thankful for WHO I am.

Thankful for WHERE I've been.

Thankful for who I am BECOMING.

Thankful for my JOURNEY.

Thankful I get to REWRITE my story.

Thankful I can SHOW UP my way.
.
Thankful I can make DECISIONS.

Thankful HAPPINESS can be mine.

Thankful for all the BEAUTY I see.

Thankful to INSPIRE others.

.

...we are already found, already truly, entirely, wildly, messily, marvelously who we were born to be.

- Anne Lamott

I AM THANKFUL FOR WHO I AM. RIGHT HERE. RIGHT NOW.

You have not been put here to just take up space.

Where you are right now is special, important, PERFECT.

.

# PROMPT #1

I am not defined by
where I am, but who I am.
I most love this about myself.

_____

_____

_____

_____

_____

_____

_____

_____

_____

# PROMPT #2

Today I will be kind to myself.
Here's how...

_____

_____

_____

_____

_____

_____

_____

_____

_____

_____

# PROMPT #3

I can choose so many moods.
Today, I choose this one,
and here's why...

_____

_____

_____

_____

_____

_____

_____

_____

_____

_____

_____

_____

# PROMPT #4

I learned so much about myself
when I was faced with...

_____

_____

_____

_____

_____

_____

_____

_____

_____

_____

_____

_____

# PROMPT #5

Every day I am evolving.
I am so thankful to have
changed in this way...

_____

_____

_____

_____

_____

_____

_____

_____

_____

_____

_____

_____

You are a child of
the universe,
no less than the trees
and the stars;
you have a right
to be here.


- Max Ehrmann

# I AM THANKFUL FOR WHERE I'VE BEEN.

Acknowledge the ups and downs. What you have LEARNED from your struggles and successes.

Know that the bumps in the road have been your teachers.

# PROMPT #6

Some of what I've been through was really difficult. But it helped me discover this about myself.

_____

_____

_____

_____

_____

_____

_____

_____

_____

_____

_____

_____

# PROMPT #7

When I look back, I always enjoy
recalling this event in my life.

_____

_____

_____

_____

_____

_____

_____

_____

_____

_____

_____

_____

# PROMPT #8

I'll never forget the time I received
this gift. It was amazing because...

_____

_____

_____

_____

_____

_____

_____

_____

_____

_____

_____

_____

# PROMPT #9

I loved this song growing up.
It made me feel...

_____

_____

_____

_____

_____

_____

_____

_____

_____

_____

_____

_____

# PROMPT #10

I will never forget this
incredible teacher for...

_____

_____

_____

_____

_____

_____

_____

_____

_____

_____

Stop worrying where
you're going, move on.

If you could know
where you're going,
you've gone.

Just keep moving on.


- Sondheim

# I Am Thankful For Who I Am Becoming

We are always evolving.
Always changing.
Always moving forward.
Toward who we are MEANT
to be.

Believe in your ability to
expand, flourish, and step
into your ultimate power.

# PROMPT #11

I love the surprises each day
brings. I look out my
window and see ...

_____

_____

_____

_____

_____

_____

_____

_____

_____

_____

_____

# PROMPT #12

I nurture myself with the people I
hang with. This one person...

_____

_____

_____

_____

_____

_____

_____

_____

_____

_____

_____

_____

# PROMPT #13

I love thinking about all the
cool things I plan to do.
Here's one of them...

_____

_____

_____

_____

_____

_____

_____

_____

_____

_____

_____

# PROMPT #14

Today I feel like describing
myself like this...

_____

_____

_____

_____

_____

_____

_____

_____

_____

_____

_____

# PROMPT #15

I am making a promise to myself
that I will...

_____

_____

_____

_____

_____

_____

_____

_____

_____

_____

_____

To see a world in a
**gr**ain **of s**and
and a **heave**n in
a wild **flower.**

**To ho**ld infinity
in the **p**alm **of yo**ur
hand. And **eter**nity
in an **hour.**

- William Blake

# I AM THANKFUL FOR MY JOURNEY.

Every STEP of your journey is a success. Even the steps that go backwards.

Your journey is a zigzag of events, not a straight line, and that is ok.

It has led you here, which is right and true.

# PROMPT #16

I am learning to forgive myself
for the time I...

_____

_____

_____

_____

_____

_____

_____

_____

_____

_____

_____

_____

# PROMPT #17

This is one experience I will
always treasure...

_____

_____

_____

_____

_____

_____

_____

_____

_____

_____

_____

# PROMPT #18

I've learned a lot so far.
This is one piece of advice
I'd say to my younger self...

_____

_____

_____

_____

_____

_____

_____

_____

_____

_____

_____

# PROMPT #19

Some of what I've been
through was really difficult.
I'm glad I had the courage to...

_____

_____

_____

_____

_____

_____

_____

_____

_____

_____

_____

# PROMPT #20

My achievements are evidence
of what I can do. I love
this particular success...

_____

_____

_____

_____

_____

_____

_____

_____

_____

_____

...forget regret, or
life is yours
to miss.

No other road,
no other way.

No day but today.

- Jonathan Larsen

# I AM THANKFUL I GET TO RE-WRITE MY STORY

Every day you get to start OVER.

Every day you get to try on different WORDS and see how they fit.

Every day is a blank page. You get to FILL it and revise as much as you want.

# PROMPT #21

Has someone helped you
along the way? What would
you say to thank them?
Write it here...

_____

_____

_____

_____

_____

_____

_____

_____

_____

_____

_____

_____

# PROMPT #22

How would you show
appreciation to yourself for
going on a "no shit-talk" diet?

_____

_____

_____

_____

_____

_____

_____

_____

_____

_____

_____

# PROMPT #23

What is something you learned that you can pass on to others?

_____

_____

_____

_____

_____

_____

_____

_____

_____

_____

_____

# PROMPT #24

Our bodies tell us what we need.
Write your body a thank-you
note for that walk, or bike ride,
or swim, or run, or nap, or...

_____

_____

_____

_____

_____

_____

_____

_____

_____

_____

# PROMPT #25

Recall a time you chose courage
over fear. What did you do?

_____
_____
_____
_____
_____
_____
_____
_____
_____
_____
_____
_____

If they don't **give yo**u a
**se**at at **the** table,
**br**in**g** a **fo**ldin**g** chair.


- Shirley Chisholm

# I AM THANKFUL I CAN SHOW UP MY WAY

You can CHOOSE
how you want to show up.

You can LET GO of old
beliefs, old stories that
were handed down to you.

They were
NEVER yours.

# PROMPT #26

So thankful I let go of this
old story...

_____

_____

_____

_____

_____

_____

_____

_____

_____

_____

_____

# PROMPT #27

Today, I thank me for...

_____

_____

_____

_____

_____

_____

_____

_____

_____

_____

_____

# PROMPT #28

All my small victories are important.
Here's one that is very meaningful...

_____

_____

_____

_____

_____

_____

_____

_____

_____

_____

_____

_____

# PROMPT #29

This friend undertands me
so well. This is how I will
show my appreciation...

_____

_____

_____

_____

_____

_____

_____

_____

_____

_____

_____

# PROMPT #30

I'm learning how to not
talk down to myself.
Here's one word (or phrase)
I will change.

_____

_____

_____

_____

_____

_____

_____

_____

_____

_____

_____

**Life is a great big canvas;**

**throw all the paint
you can at it.**

-Danny Kaye

# I AM THANKFUL I CAN MAKE DECISIONS.

Knowing what you want and making a decision to go after it is POWERFUL.
That takes guts.

It means taking ACTIONS and being 100% responsible for the outcomes.

# PROMPT #31

It was scary to make this
decision, but worth it. This is why
I am so thankful I did...

_____

_____

_____

_____

_____

_____

_____

_____

_____

_____

# PROMPT #32

What do you want to say yes to?
Can you see it? Feel it?
Describe it here.

_____

_____

_____

_____

_____

_____

_____

_____

_____

_____

_____

# PROMPT #33

When I quiet my mind, this is
what I dream about doing...

_____

_____

_____

_____

_____

_____

_____

_____

_____

_____

_____

# PROMPT #34

What is something special you
never thought you'd have? How
can you express thanks for it?

_____

_____

_____

_____

_____

_____

_____

_____

_____

_____

_____

# PROMPT #35

What do you want to say no to?
Can you see it? Feel it?
Describe it here.

_____

_____

_____

_____

_____

_____

_____

_____

_____

_____

_____

_____

_____

It is **never too** late
to be what **yo**u
mi**ght have bee**n.

-George Eliot

# I AM THANKFUL
# HAPPINESS
# CAN BE MINE.

You need only look,
and ALLOW...

Beauty into your life.
Joy into your life.
Laughter into your life.
Kindness into your life.
Grace into your life.

# PROMPT #36

Because I took this chance,
my life...

_____
_____
_____
_____
_____
_____
_____
_____
_____
_____
_____
_____

# PROMPT #37

When I let my mind wander.
this is what I dream I can be...

_____

_____

_____

_____

_____

_____

_____

_____

_____

_____

_____

_____

# PROMPT #38

There is only Hell Yes & Hell No.
(There is no Hell Maybe). I am
so thankful I said Hell Yes to this...

_____

_____

_____

_____

_____

_____

_____

_____

_____

_____

_____

# PROMPT #39

What are you thankful for,
right now?

_____

_____

_____

_____

_____

_____

_____

_____

_____

_____

_____

# PROMPT #40

I am so grateful for the
happiness I feel when...

_____

_____

_____

_____

_____

_____

_____

_____

_____

_____

_____

# Shower the people you love with love...

-James Taylor

# I AM THANKFUL FOR ALL THE BEAUTY I SEE

You can choose to see the world as magical.

You can let in your life the magic around you.

It's all here for you.

# PROMPT #41

I am so thankful you showed me
this beauty in the world...

_____

_____

_____

_____

_____

_____

_____

_____

_____

_____

_____

# PROMPT #42

The world is here for me and nothing
is impossible. Today, I am especially
thankful for...

_____

_____

_____

_____

_____

_____

_____

_____

_____

_____

# PROMPT #43

I remind myself that I am part
of this beautiful world.
And, I feel grateful for...

_____

_____

_____

_____

_____

_____

_____

_____

_____

_____

_____

# PROMPT #44

The stillness of nature teaches me
to look, observe, and appreciate. Today, I
am surprised and delighted by....

_____

_____

_____

_____

_____

_____

_____

_____

_____

# PROMPT #45

I can get so lost in problems, but I find this to be thankful for today.

_____

_____

_____

_____

_____

_____

_____

_____

_____

_____

**Your playing small
doesn't serve
the world.**

-Marianne Williamson

I AM THANKFUL I CAN INSPIRE OTHERS.

ALLOW yourself to embrace your unique self, talents, and awesome ideas.

YOU will inspire someone to do great things, and APPRECIATE their life.

# PROMPT #46

I didn't think this was very special, but now I truly appreciate this about myself.

_____

_____

_____

_____

_____

_____

_____

_____

_____

_____

# PROMPT #47

You make me feel like I matter.
Thank you for cheering me on when...

_____

_____

_____

_____

_____

_____

_____

_____

_____

_____

# PROMPT #48

You helped me step out and be who
I am. Your support means...

_____

_____

_____

_____

_____

_____

_____

_____

_____

_____

_____

# PROMPT #49

I cannot stop saying thank you for the
laughter you brought into my life.
I remember the time...

_____

_____

_____

_____

_____

_____

_____

_____

_____

_____

_____

# PROMPT #50

These are just some of the amazing
adjectives that describe you...

_____

_____

_____

_____

_____

_____

_____

_____

_____

_____

# PROMPT #51

I have a lot to offer.
And I am grateful I am able
to share this with others...

_____

_____

_____

_____

_____

_____

_____

_____

_____

_____

# PROMPT #52

Every morning and every evening
I thank the world for....

_____

_____

_____

_____

_____

_____

_____

_____

_____

_____

Be present
in all things
and thankful
for all things.

-Maya Angelou

www.ingramcontent.com/pod-product-compliance
Lightning Source LLC
Chambersburg PA
CBHW071518120626
46550CB00006B/2260

* 9 7 9 8 2 1 8 0 0 4 5 3 8 *